GOLDEN DAYS

GOLDEN DAYS

Historic Photographs of the London Zoo

With a Foreword by

Professor Lord Zuckerman OM KCB FRS

Honorary Secretary
the Zoological Society of London

DUCKWORTH

First published in 1976 by
Gerald Duckworth & Co. Ltd.
The Old Piano Factory,
43 Gloucester Crescent, London NW1.

Cloth ISBN 0 7156 1063 5

Paper ISBN 0 7156 1134 8

Designed by Patrick Leeson

Printed in Great Britain by
Page Bros (Norwich) Ltd, Norwich

Foreword

In the archives of the Zoological Society of London there are some 15,000 half- and quarter-plate glass photographic negatives. Many of them are the work of F. W. Bond, an accountant who joined the Society's staff in 1903. Mr Bond, whom I knew well, was an enthusiastic and accomplished animal photographer, and most of the pictures in this book are his. They show the London Zoo as it was between the Wars, and I have no doubt that they will bring back happy memories to all who, as children, visited the Zoo at that time.

From its earliest days, the Zoological Society has been a pioneer in improving methods of animal husbandry and in the development of buildings for exotic animals. Not surprisingly, there have been great changes since the photographs reproduced in this book were taken. Enclosures have taken the place of Victorian buildings which new knowledge has shown to be inadequate for their inmates. Cages containing single, lonely creatures have been torn down and, whenever possible, animals are kept in space which gives room for play and in which breeding groups can multiply. Diets have improved and feeding by the public has stopped. All this has resulted in better health, and a big decrease in the transmission of infectious disease.

There is a growing public distaste for exhibitions in which the natural dignity of an animal is destroyed by dressing it up, or by making it do tricks. No zoo should have the aspect of a circus, and this has always been avoided by the Zoological Society of London, within the constraints of current fashion, and in the fulfilment of its purpose, as laid down in its Charter in 1829, to advance Zoology and Animal Physiology and to introduce 'new and curious subjects of the Animal Kingdom'. There is little, if any, excuse now for keeping wild animals in captivity unless every opportunity is taken to study them scientifically and to breed them, especially those that are endangered by the spread of human population. Two of the animals shown in this book, the quagga and the thylacine (p. 59), are already extinct. In the London Zoo of today, they might well have survived.

A look into the past, which is what these photographs present, helps us to assess how far we have progressed.

Professor Lord Zuckerman, OM KCB FRS

Honorary Secretary, The Zoological Society of London

Acknowledgements

Photography: research and preparation
T. B. Dennett (*Research Photographer*)

Compilation, selection and captions
L. G. Goodwin (*Director of Science*)
R. D. Martin (*Senior Research Fellow*)

With advice from
H. G. Vevers (*Assistant Director of Science*)
M. R. Brambell (*Curator of Mammals*)
P. J. S. Olney (*Curator of Birds*)
R. A. Fish (*Librarian*)

Identification of Zoo staff
E. B. Tanner (*Overseer of Birds, retired*)
H. Corbett (*Senior Pathology Technician, retired*)

Gratitude is expressed to the Pilgrim Trust for a grant towards the expenses of preservation and reorganization of photographic archives.

NOTES ON THE PHOTOGRAPHERS AND THEIR EQUIPMENT

Frederick William Bond (1887–1942) joined the Zoological Society's Accounts Department in 1903. He served in the Army from 1917 to 1919 and after he was demobilised was appointed Accountant. He later became the Society's Assistant Treasurer. He made a vast collection of photographs, which were presented to the Society on his death

Frederick Martin Duncan (1873–1961) was the son of Professor Peter Martin Duncan, a famous geologist and naturalist. He had done research in marine biology and agricultural entomology before he was appointed Clerk of Publications and Librarian to the Zoological Society in 1919. He was an expert photographer and a pioneer in applying cinematography to invertebrates and microscopic creatures

David Seth-Smith (1875–1963) studied as a civil engineer and architect, but devoted much of his time to natural history. He served on the Council of the Zoological Society 1906–1909; went to Australia on the Society's behalf in 1907. He was awarded the Society's silver medal in 1908. In 1919 he joined the Society's staff as Curator of Mammals and Birds and was well known as the 'Zoo Man' of the BBC 'Children's Hour'

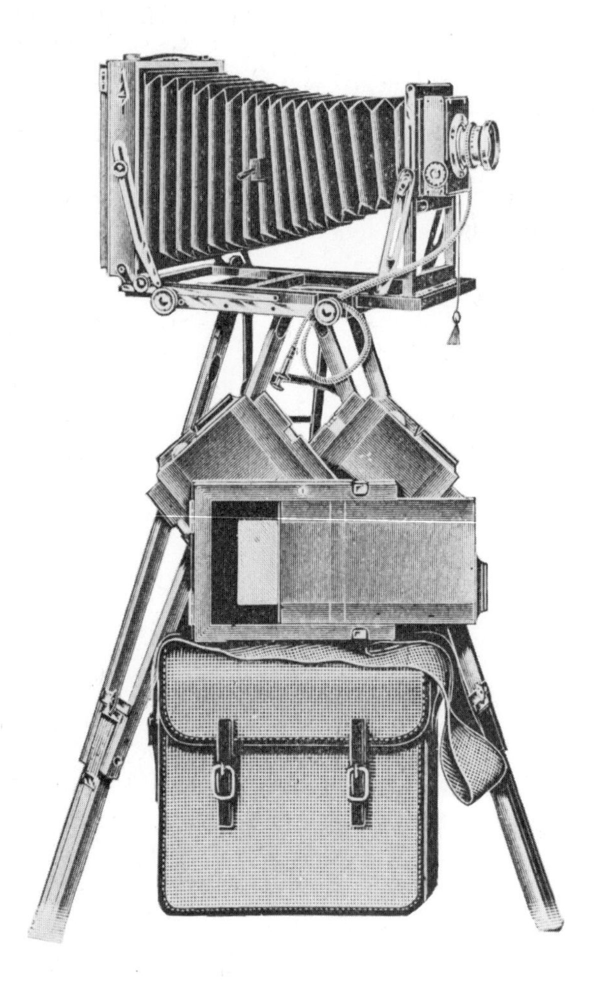

Figure 1(a) Half-plate camera outfit, early 1900s

Figure 1(b) Half-plate camera (1908) Thornton-Pickard 'Royal Ruby'

MOST OF THE photographs in this book were taken with a 'single lens reflex' camera. Equipment of this type offers special advantages to the animal photographer since the final image may be observed directly on the focussing screen, right up to the moment of exposure. Direct reflex viewing also makes sharpness and correct focus easy to achieve, and the rapid focal plane shutter fitted to these cameras enables the required pose and expression to be captured the instant it is seen.

F. W. Bond, who is the main contributor of pictures to this book, began his photography with a half-plate ($6\frac{1}{2}'' \times 4\frac{3}{4}''$) stand camera (fig. 1a & b), but soon changed to a quarter-plate ($3\frac{1}{4}'' \times 4\frac{1}{4}''$) reflex (fig. 2), which he continued to use for almost forty years. Martin Duncan and Seth-Smith used a variety of cameras, including the Leica and a V.P. Exacta. Like many of his contemporaries, Bond preferred glass plate negatives and Pyro-Soda, a developer still considered by many to produce exquisite gradation and quality, but notorious for its poor keeping properties and ability to stain negatives, fingers and fabrics a deep yellow. Bond's favourite plates during his early years appear to have been Ilford 'Zenith' and Wellington and Ward's 'Xtra speedy press plates' (with a speed roughly equivalent to about ASA 10), which required an exposure in sunlight of 1/100 sec at f4.5 or 1/15 sec during dull weather—a far cry from today's 'Xtra speedy' Tri X film which allows sunlight exposures of 1/1000 sec at f11, and may be used at 1/500 at f4 even in dull weather.

Slow speed films and uncertain developers were not the only problem confronting the animal photographer of the period; he was also faced with the task of finding correct exposures under rapidly varying light conditions with the limited technical means available. Four choices were open to the photographer in the early 1900s; he could guess the exposure, use an exposure table, an extinction meter or an actinometer.

The 'guess' method was not favoured by many serious photographers, because a great number of exposures had to be made in order to gain experience in judging lighting conditions. Users of this method usually kept to one type of plate and worked at a pre-set shutter speed or lens stop.

The second choice, the *exposure table*, also partly based on the guessing principle, was a distinct advantage, as trial testing was carried out by scientifically trained investigators who averaged the results of years of data on lighting conditions and plate speeds, condensing the information into a simple chart.

Figure 2 Quarter-plate single lens reflex 'Ensign Popular', early 1900s

The third and fourth choices were both mechanical devices designed to give an estimate of the exposure by actually measuring the existing light. The extinction photometer (fig. 3)—essentially a viewing tube containing a row of numbers of steadily increasing density—gave the correct exposure factor when the darkest number could still be seen under the prevailing lighting conditions, and was used in conjunction with a table or calculator. The actinometer (fig. 4) worked on a similar principle, but employed a piece of self-darkening photographic paper to measure the strength of the light. Another stratagem adopted by many photographers (and probably the one adopted by Bond) was to use the camera itself as an extinction meter by observing the subject on the ground glass screen and then closing the lens aperture until the shadow detail was no longer visible. After a few test exposures this method produces quite accurate results and is very rapid in use; it is still employed by a few studio photographers today.

All these methods worked well in average conditions, but were renowned for their unreliability when used under the uncustomary circumstances found in the Zoo. The actinometer when used in an animal house like the Lion House needed a full five minutes to darken to the required tint.

Despite these difficulties, Bond—working only in his spare time—managed to produce over 5,000 negatives which were sharp, well exposed and pictorially interesting.

T. B. Dennett
Research Photographer, Zoological Society of London

Figure 3 Early exposure photometer

Figure 4 Watkins Bee Meter. Early exposure meter employing self-darkening photographic paper

Above Komodo dragon 'Sumbawa', with keeper Budd (1928). The scar on the reptile's neck was caused by a crocodile bite. On its death, the animal was taken by the British Museum (Natural History) for exhibition. *Right* Gorilla, 'Jan D. II', imitating its keeper (1925)

Keeper Martin Flewin with Peter, a tame wolf (1935)

Above Keeper Edward Lawrence massaging the chest of chimp 'Johnnie' with camphorated oil (1923)

Keeper Flewin boxing with a kangaroo (1921)

Camel lawn-mower, ridden by keeper Fred Perry (1913)

Monkey grooming keeper Flewin's head (1928)

Taking a swarm of bees (1926)

Indian elephant bathing (1926). Keeper Charles Eyles stands ready to scrub with his broom

Trimming Indian elephant's feet (1926). It is not easy to give enough exercise on rough ground to produce natural 'wear', and trimming – like cutting our own fingernails – is sometimes needed. This is still done today

Arrival of baby elephants (1914). The two keepers on the right are Harry Robertson and Charles Eyles

Left Keepers oiling the African elephant 'Kiberinge' to prevent skin cracks (1927)

Above Young African elephants 'Jumbo II' and 'Hango' (1934)

Elephants passing King's Cross station on the way to the Zoo in 1927. They had walked from the London docks

Indian elephant with its keeper before the Second World War

Right White elephant, with Dr Saw Po Min and his son (1926)

Left and right Sayaid Ali and the Indian elephant 'Indiarani' (1922)

Below Burmese elephants (1923). The keeper on the right is Jack Milbourne, the turbaned man on the left Sayaid Ali and the man in the centre San Dwe, who taught his elephants to play the mouth organ. Sayaid Ali and San Dwe were elephant trainers and one day in 1927, during a quarrel, San Dwe killed Sayaid Ali with a pick-axe. The murderer was sentenced but was not executed.

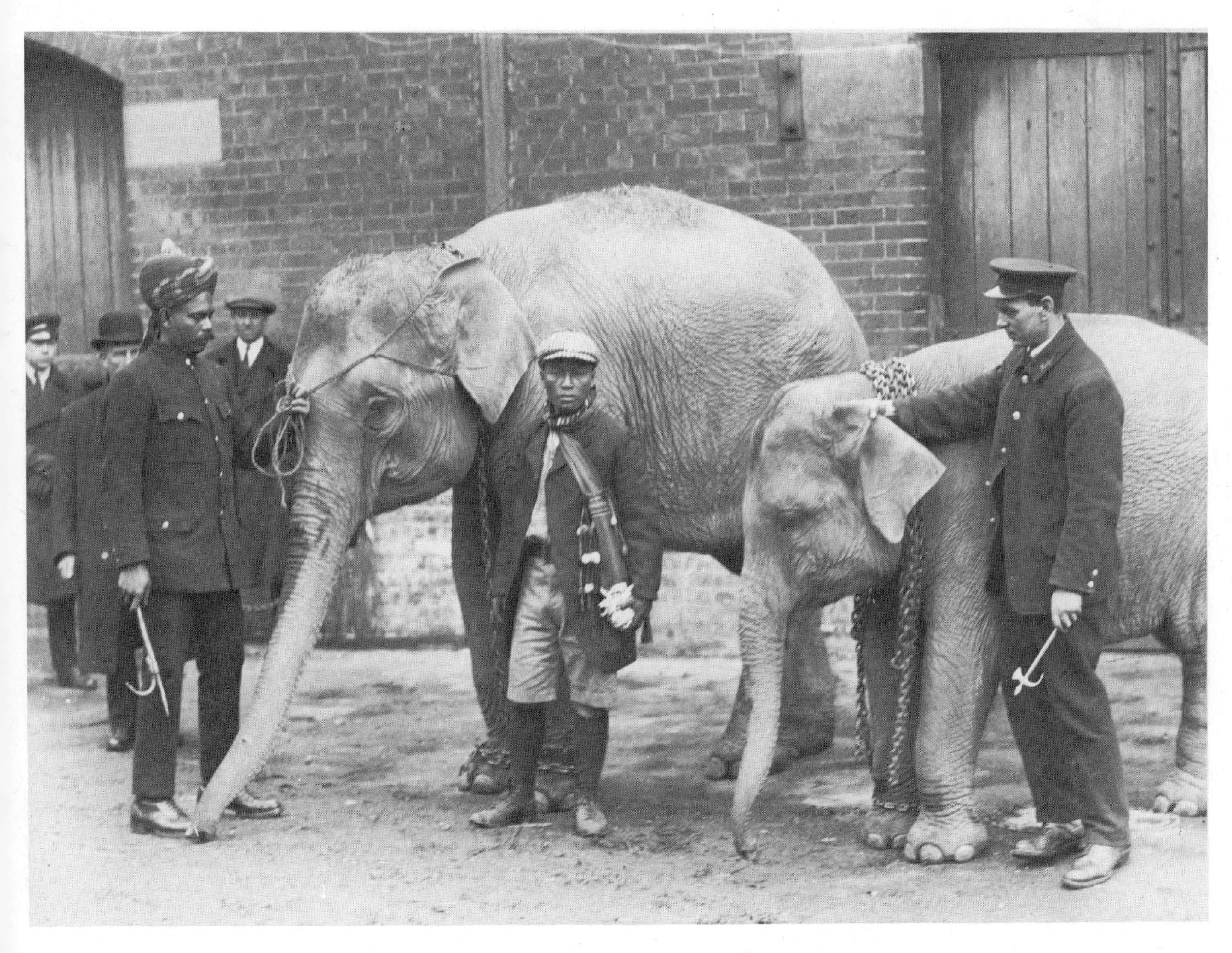

Indian rhinoceros in its paddock (1913)

Polar bear taking a dose of cod-liver oil (1914)

A drink for a polar bear provided by head gardener Mark Edwards (1914)

'Sam' the polar bear begging for food (1912)

Keeper Arthur Chandler giving cod-liver oil to a walrus (1923). Such haphazard dosing does not occur nowadays. The oil soluble vitamins A & D are incorporated in the prepared food so that the correct amount is given

Keeper Ernie Bowman and 'Bobbie' (1923)

Keeper Ernie Bowman, with hippos 'Joan' and 'Jimmy' (1927)

Pygmy hippopotamus (1913). This animal, which is now restricted to certain regions of Liberia and Sierra Leone, is less attached to water than its larger relative the common hippopotamus

Keeper Ernie Bowman feeding a young pygmy hippopotamus (1923)

Keeper Ernie Bowman, with hippos 'Bobbie' and 'Joan' (1923)

A grizzly bear wallowing in its pool (1924). The photograph must have been taken at a relatively rapid exposure to show the reflections from the water surface so distinctly

A sea-lion eager for its meal of fish (1924). This photograph was taken with a telephoto lens at full aperture

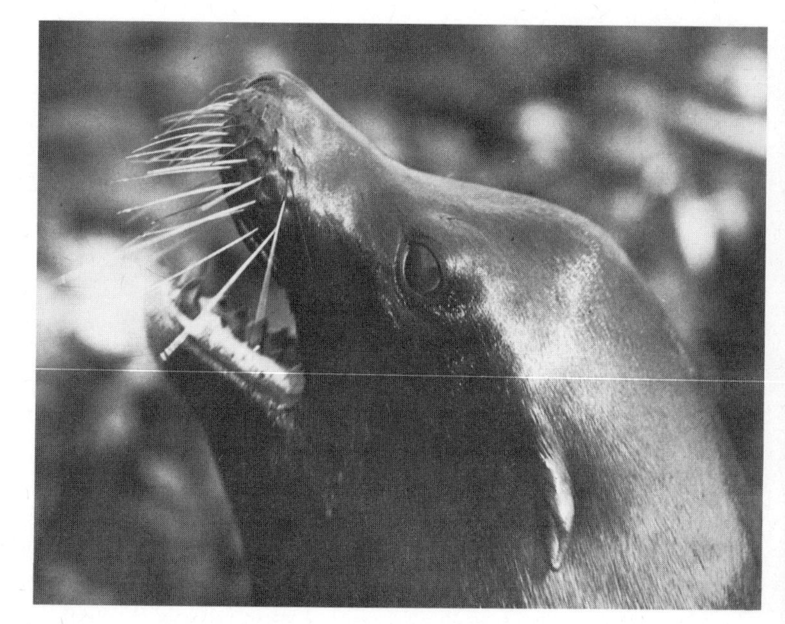

A brown bear on the Mappin Terrace (1927)

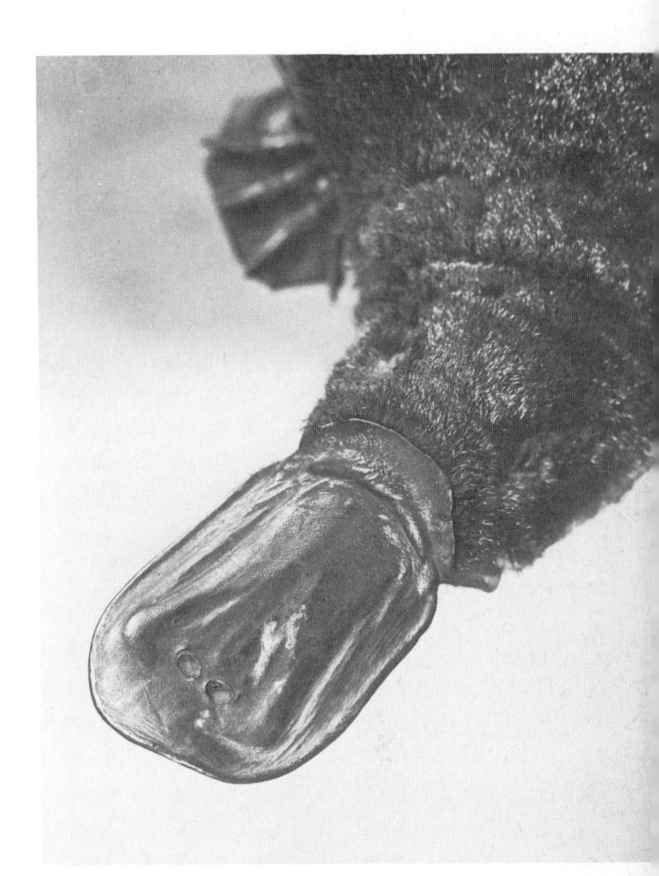

A duck-billed platypus, one of the two surviving types of egg-laying mammal (1928)

A green turtle, weighing 4 cwt., photographed in the existing aquarium (1933)

The Ant Palace, a display-case imported from America (1936)

Close-up view of an ant (1938)

A lantern-fly of the family Fulgoridae (1927). The strange appendage on the head is a device to confuse predators

Jackson's horned chameleon from Kenya (1926). This photograph was probably taken in the special photographic cage shown on p. 46

Alligators in a cage with scenic background (1928)

A giant toad in the hands of a keeper (1923)

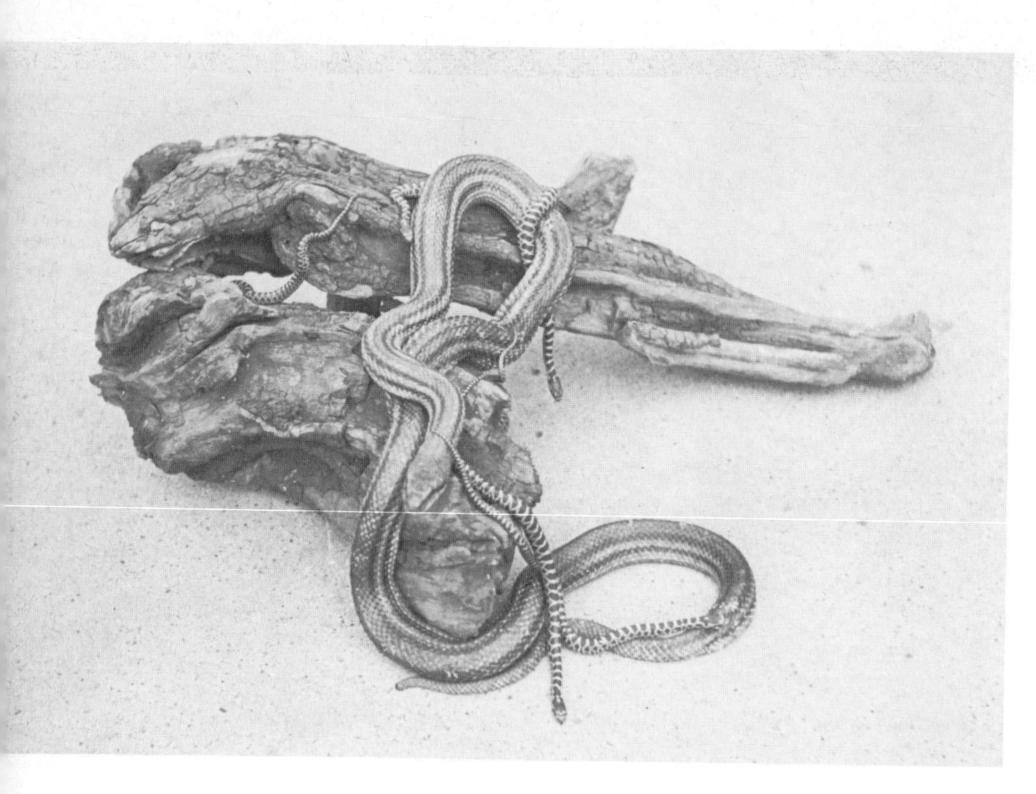

Female four line snake and offspring (1938)

Stocktaking the reptiles (1935). Keepers Dexter and Wilson

A pelican after a meal of 17 herrings, showing how the gular pouch can be distended for a large volume of fish (1922)

Portrait of a barn owl, showing its heart-shaped facial disc (1928). The forward-facing eyes permit a considerable degree of binocular vision, essential in hunting prey

The camouflage coloration and characteristic, slightly raised posture of the tawny frogmouth merge perfectly in the lichen-covered trees of its natural habitat (1921)

Lesser egret in breeding plumage (1928). During fashionable plume-wearing days in Victorian and Edwardian times, thousands of egrets were slaughtered for their feathers. Changes in fashion and in the law saved these birds from extinction

Shoebill, or whale-headed stork (1926). This swamp-living bird from East Africa can reach a height of up to 4 feet and uses its massive bill to eat a wide range of animal prey

Vulture from Pondicherry in India (1922). The bare skin of the head permits feeding on carrion without soiling the feathers with blood

A flying fox, or fruit-bat, taking its usual upside-down view of its surroundings (1939)

King penguin, with keeper Harry Munro (1914). Munro was killed in the First World War, having served in the army, in airships and on anti-submarine patrol

The large eyes of this slender loris (1926) betray its exclusively nocturnal habits. This photograph was probably taken in the special cage illustrated on p. 46

The changeable hawk-eagle of South East Asia (1923)

Jackass penguins (1924) in the kennel-like nest-boxes formerly used for penguins at the London Zoo

Lion cubs (presented by Sir Geoffrey Archer): 'Abdullah' and 'Fatima' carried by keepers Fred Woolston and William Hopgood (1921)

A caracal in aggressive mood (1924)

Lion sleeping (1924).

A lion photographed at Whipsnade with a half-plate camera in 1935

A baby leopard just after a feed (1915)

Chimpanzee picking keeper Shelley's pocket (1934)

Keeper Shelley with chimps (1927)

'John' the gorilla (1919)

The gorilla 'Meng' (1939)

Chimpanzee taking cod-liver oil (1923)

Chimpanzee watching the spectators (1921)

16
15
14
13
12
11
10
9
8
7
6
5
4

The Giraffe House (1928) with a convenient scale for those interested in statistics. This is one of the few early buildings still in use today

Giant anteater *(Myrmecophaga tridactyla)* from South America. The foreleg closely resembles the head of a carnivore, and this may help to protect the animal from predators in its natural habitat (1923)

The ostrich is the world's largest living bird, reaching a height of up to 8 feet and a weight of up to 350 lb. It also has a habit of eating a miscellaneous range of objects in captivity (1914)

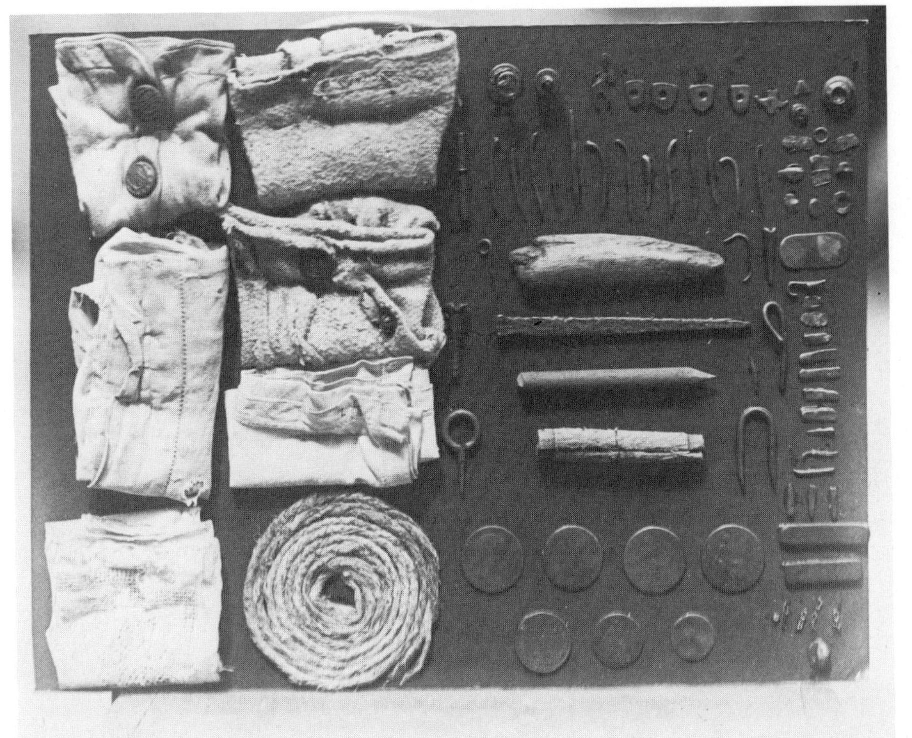

A collection of objects found in the stomach of an ostrich at post mortem in 1927 – coins, staples, screws, nuts, rope, and even shirts. Before feeding of animals by the public was stopped, deaths quite often occurred

This Mazawattee Tea cart (1914), drawn by a team of zebras, was one of the London Zoo's early advertising devices. The building in the background is the main office of the Zoological Society, virtually as it is today

Some privileged visitors to the giraffe enclosure in 1926

'Betty' on a tortoise (1924)

Armenians in the llama cart with keeper (1923)

Keeper Alf Taylor keeping a watchful eye on a young visitor taking a camel ride (1922)

A llama cart transporting visitors (1923)

Above August bank holiday at the London Zoo in 1922. 47,578 people visited the zoo on that day

Elephant riding (1936). The four 'mahouts' are keepers Bailey, Cullen, Milbourn and Jones

King George V and Queen Mary opening the aquarium – April 1924

Visit of Haile Selassie of Abyssinia (Ethiopia) at the time of the British Empire Exhibition in 1924. The Secretary of the Zoological Society, Sir Peter Chalmers Mitchell, is wearing the silk hat

Right and far right Visit of Victor Emmanuel, King of Italy, during the British Empire Exhibition in 1924. On the King's left is Dr. Geoffrey Vevers, Superintendent of the Gardens from 1923 to 1948

Below King penguins and some smaller jackass penguins at feeding time, with keepers White and Doubleday, watched by H.R.H. Princess Elizabeth and H.R.H. Princess Margaret (June, 1939)

During the official visit of H.R.H. Princess Elizabeth and H.R.H. Princess Margaret to the London Zoo in June 1939, pony-rides were among the events organised. Princess Margaret is shown riding one of the ponies

Mongolian wild ass used for riding. The keeper is Bill Milne (1914)

Below Mr and Mrs Martin Johnson (1920) with an orang-utan and a gibbon. Johnson was a pioneer of animal films in Africa; his wife was friendly with the pygmies

Cowgirls on a camel, with keeper Arthur Page (1924)

'Ming', one of the first giant pandas kept at the London Zoo, enjoying a ride through the grounds (1939)

The south entrance to the Zoological Society's Gardens, photographed in 1927. The enlargement provides a good illustration of the effects of inflation. The photograph was taken with a large plate camera (of half-plate size)

A view of the Camel House, designed by Decimus Burton soon after the foundation of thc Zoological Society. The clock tower, photographed in 1928, still exists

A cage for still photographs of small vertebrates and invertebrates used by F. W. Bond (1928). Such apparatus was useful not only for isolating individual animals to take portrait photographs, but also for taking close-up and sequence photographs for scientific study

Transporting animals. The solid-tyred Thorneycroft is driven by Mr Fred Abbott (1921)

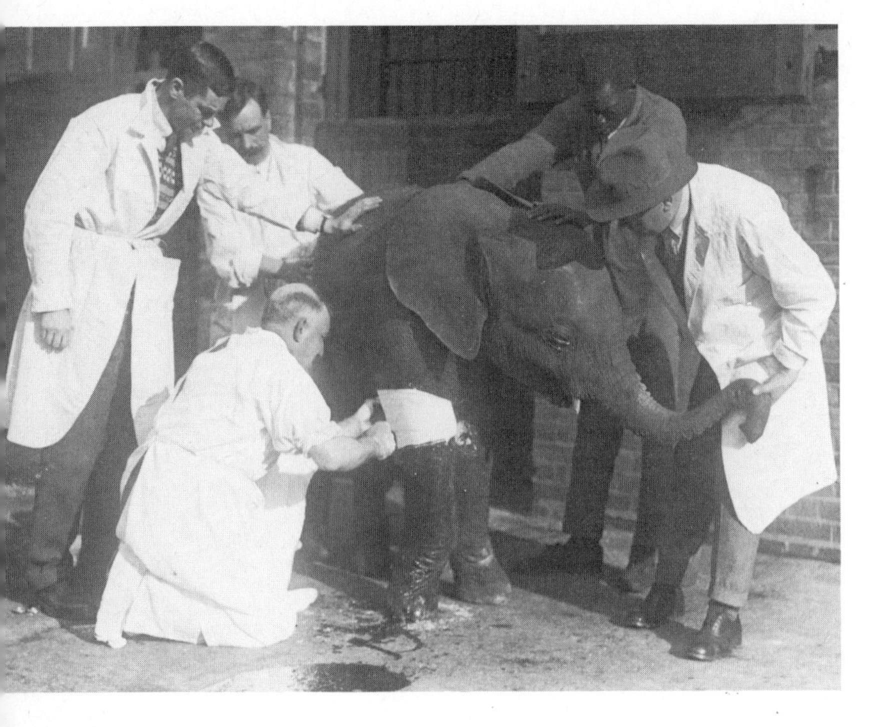

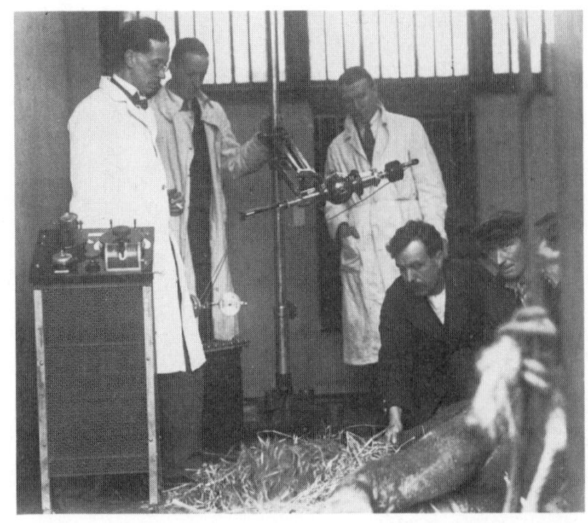

Above left Pygmy African elephant 'Oojah' having plaster fixed to a splint (December 1925), attended by keepers Warwick and Hicks. This photograph was taken on an unbacked plate. When negative emulsions are coated on clear film or glass plates, the light is transmitted through the emulsion and reflected, causing dense flare around the highlights. This is known as 'halation' and is usually prevented by coating the back of the unexposed negative with a dark, water-soluble paint

Above right Using an early design of x-ray machine to examine an injured elephant's leg (1926). Standing to the right of the machine is Billy Lawrence, and kneeling in front of him is keeper Warwick. The radiation scatter from such an x-ray tube was considerable

Construction of the existing Mappin Terrace in 1912. Photographer unknown – copy from $3\frac{1}{4}$ inch square lantern slide

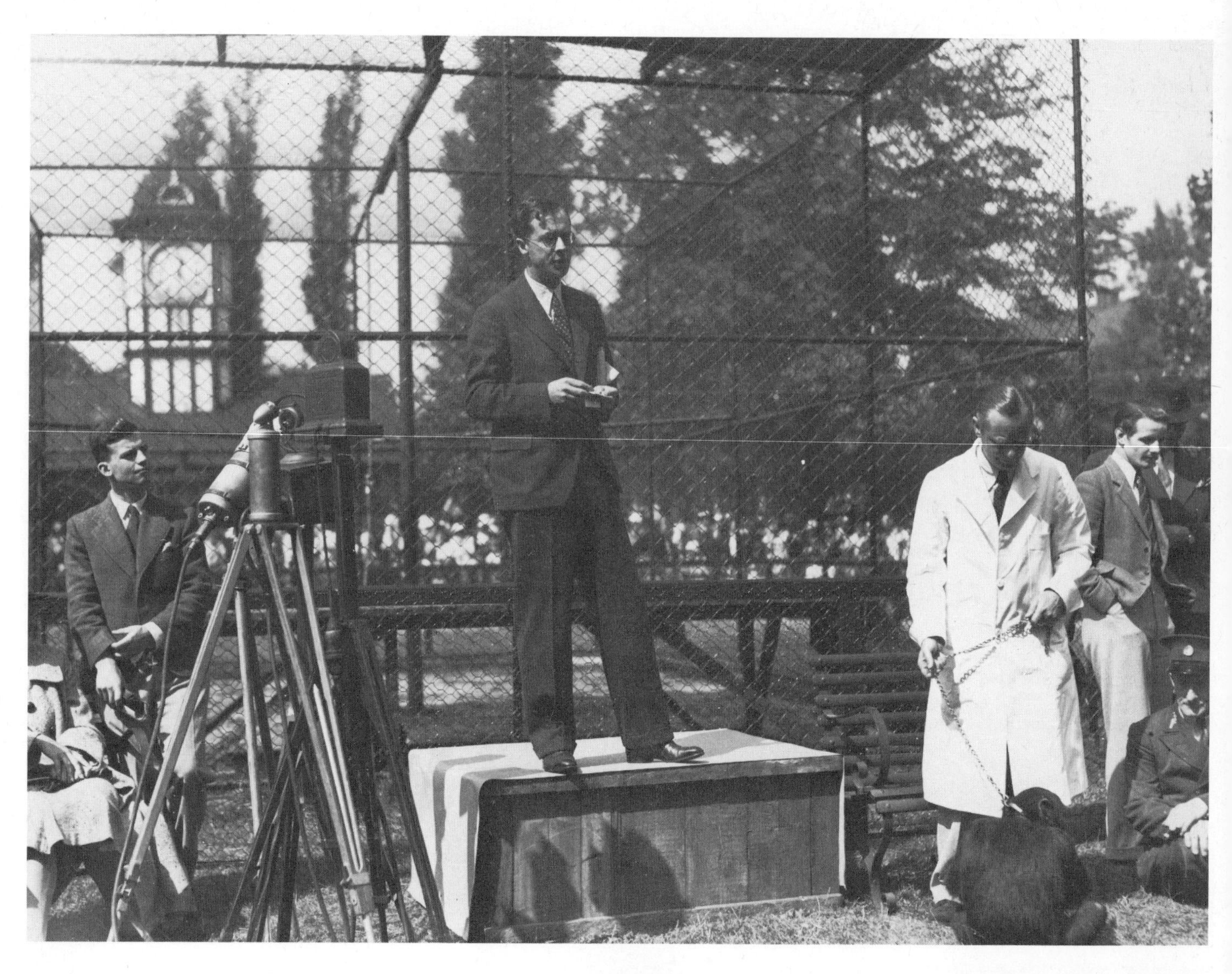

The late Sir Julian Huxley, a former Secretary of the Zoological Society, officially opening Pets' Corner in August 1935

The event was closely followed by both still photographers and 'cine men' for news coverage. A single-lens reflex camera of the type used by F. W. Bond, but not by the earlier photographers, can be seen in the hands of the photographer second from the left in the front row

The rat-catcher (1920)

A goat in the sweet shop (1914)

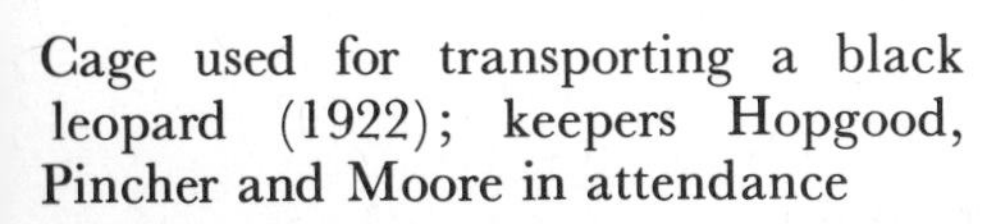

Cage used for transporting a black leopard (1922); keepers Hopgood, Pincher and Moore in attendance

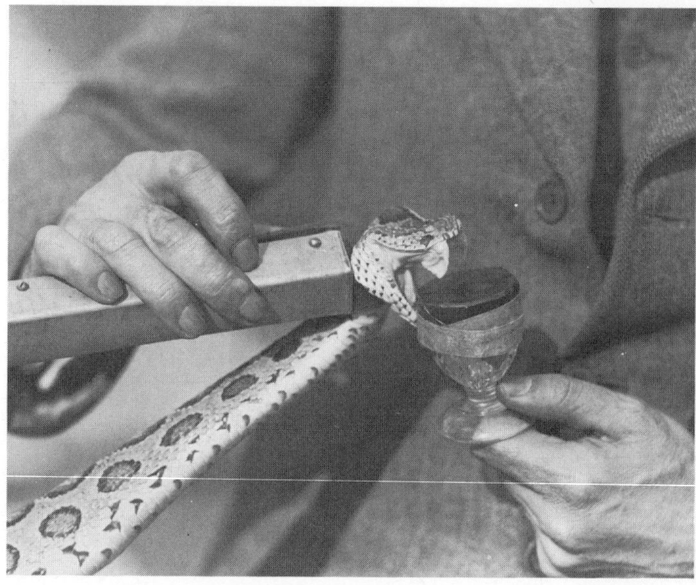

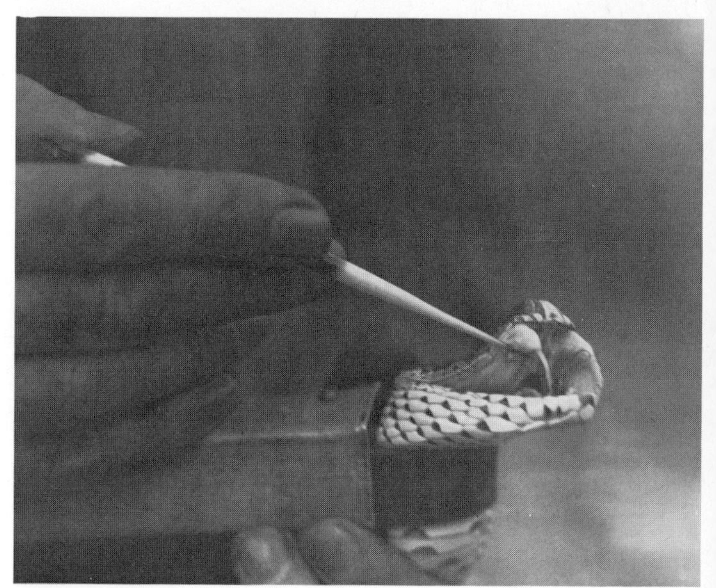

Keeper Arthur Budd working with a Russell's viper (1934). Venom was formerly collected from Russell's vipers for experimental work on blood clotting. After the viper had been firmly locked in a holding stick, it was made to strike at a wine glass covered with oiled silk. The venom collected in the glass was then used in the experimental apparatus shown. The venom is still used to measure one of the factors that cause blood to clot – an important test in diseases of the heart and arteries

David Seth-Smith (the BBC 'Zoo Man' and also a keen zoo photographer), blowing an ostrich egg (1922). He is assisted by G. R. Doubleday, seen on the right, and in the photograph below

These two tigers are photographed here at Whipsnade in a natural setting somewhat unusual for the period (1935). Nowadays, breeding of tigers in captivity has become relatively commonplace

Two baby pumas (1938). This is one of the rare occasions when F. W. Bond used a flash in his animal photography

Adjutant storks in their characteristic resting posture (1923). Despite their grotesque appearance on the ground, they are magnificent in flight

Pike in an Aquarium (1932). Photograph taken with a Sashalite flashbulb unit

This pair of hippos, 'Bobbie' and 'Joan', was photographed by the Hippo Pool in 1923

Two polar bears romping in the pool (1926)

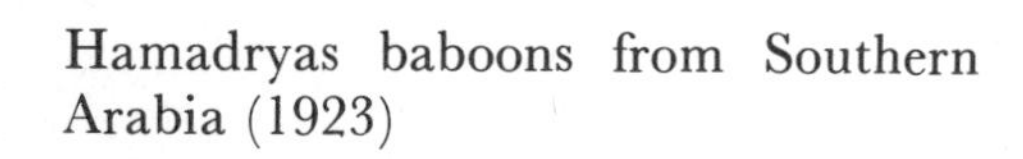

Hamadryas baboons from Southern Arabia (1923)

Grevy's zebra, mother and 4-day-old foal (1927). This is the largest of all the zebras and differs from the other types in that it lives in quite small groups in East Africa. The photograph provides an example of the good definition which could be achieved with pyro developer. The individual hairs on the mane are clearly visible on the negative

A langur mother with her infant (1913). These leaf-eating monkeys are still among the most difficult to breed in captivity, and it is likely that the mother arrived at the London Zoo already pregnant

Two young chimpanzees, 'Boo-boo' and 'Bibi' (1927)

Destruction of natural habitats and hunting have already led to the extinction of several animal species; many more are threatened. Some of the animals illustrated here are already extinct in the wild, and others may disappear by the end of the century

The giant panda has always been a favourite with visitors to the London Zoo, and it was eventually chosen by the World Wildlife Fund as its emblem. 'Ming', shown in this photograph taken in 1939, was no exception in terms of public appeal

Orang-utans (*Pongo pygmaeus*) are now becoming quite rare in their natural ranges in the rain-forests of South East Asia. The London Zoo has long kept orangs for public display, and has achieved considerable breeding successes in recent years. This male, 'Sandy', was photographed in 1916

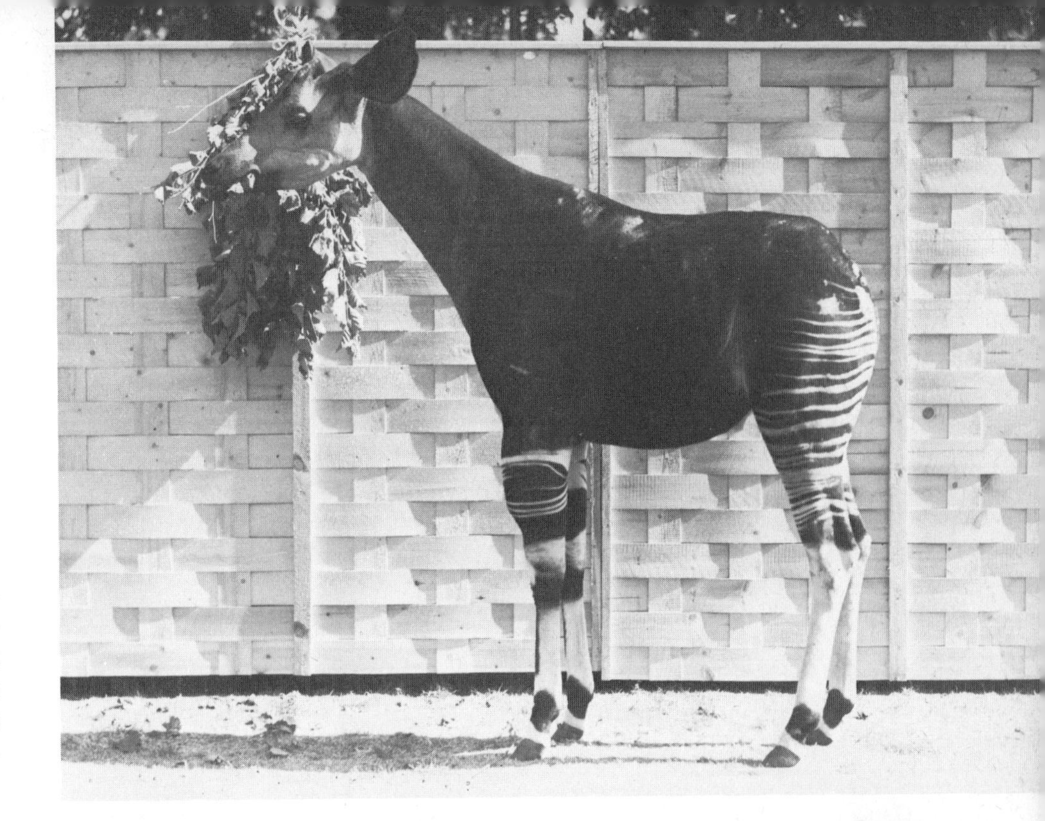

The okapi (*Okapia johnstoni*) is an inhabitant of the dense equatorial rainforests of the Congo region. It was not discovered until 1901, although it is fairly common. The knob-like horns betray its relationship to the plains-living giraffe (1935)

An album of photographs entitled 'The Zoo, *ca.* 1910' contained this rare print of a Sumatran rhinoceros (*Didermocerus sumatrensis*). The wild population of these forest-living rhinoceroses is now greatly endangered, largely because of hunters collecting horns. This photograph was taken on a 5 inch wide roll film. All early film negatives were made of unstable cellulose nitrate, which is prone to turn yellow and decompose to give a sticky substance which may ignite spontaneously if films are stored in bulk

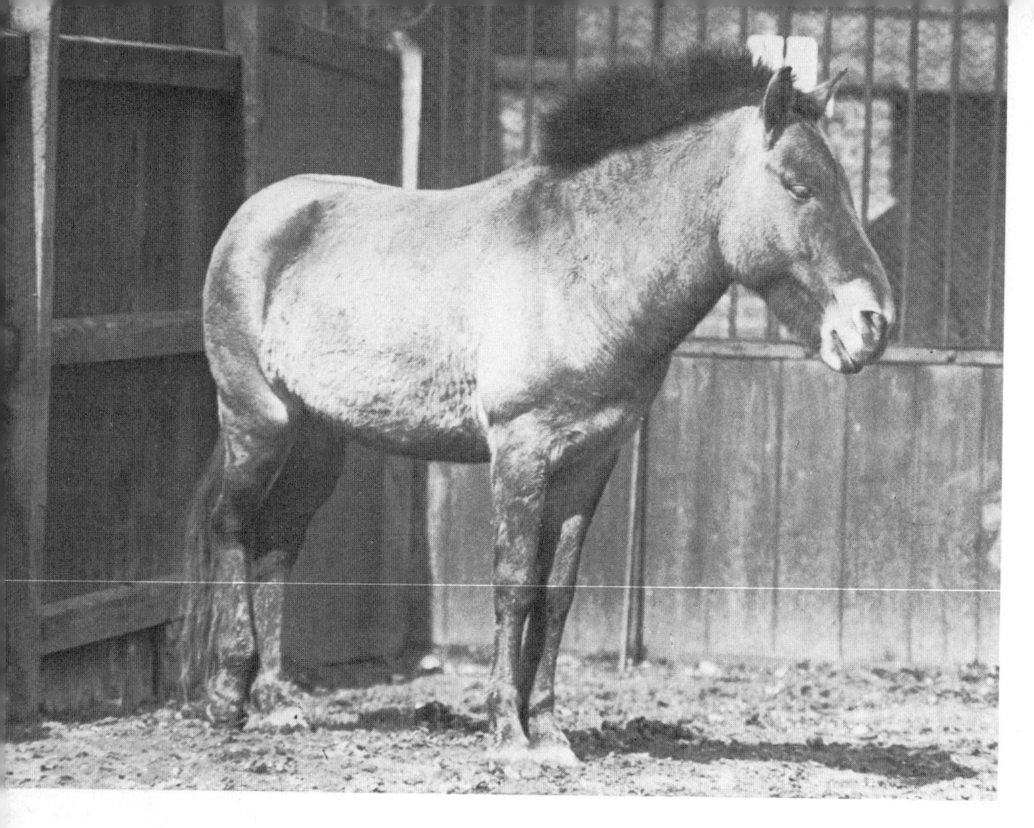

The Mongolian wild horse (*Equus przewalskii*) better known as the Przewalski horse, is the sole surviving wild relative of the domestic horse. It was described in 1881, and colonies were established in captivity at the beginning of this century. Since it is probably extinct in its natural range, the present-day stock at Whipsnade Park is one of the few surviving groups left to show the origins of domestic horses (1927)

The takin (*Budorcas taxicolor*), a rugged-looking relative of the musk-ox, is now a rare inhabitant of mountain forests in southern Asia (April 1923)

The Tasmanian pouched 'wolf' or thylacine (*Thylacinus cynocephalus*) (1913), formerly common in forested areas of Tasmania, may now be extinct. The last recorded wild specimen was shot and killed in 1930, though some apparent traces of an individual were found in a trap in 1961

This strange creature, half-way in appearance between a zebra and an ass, was known as the quagga (*Equus quagga*). It once inhabited Southern Africa, but the last survivors in the wild were wiped out by 1860. Although small numbers were kept alive for some time in captivity, the last recorded quagga died in Artis Magistra Zoo of Amsterdam in 1883. The last quagga in London Zoo died in 1872. Very few photographs of this extinct species are now available. Photo from copy of a negative taken between 1840 and 1860

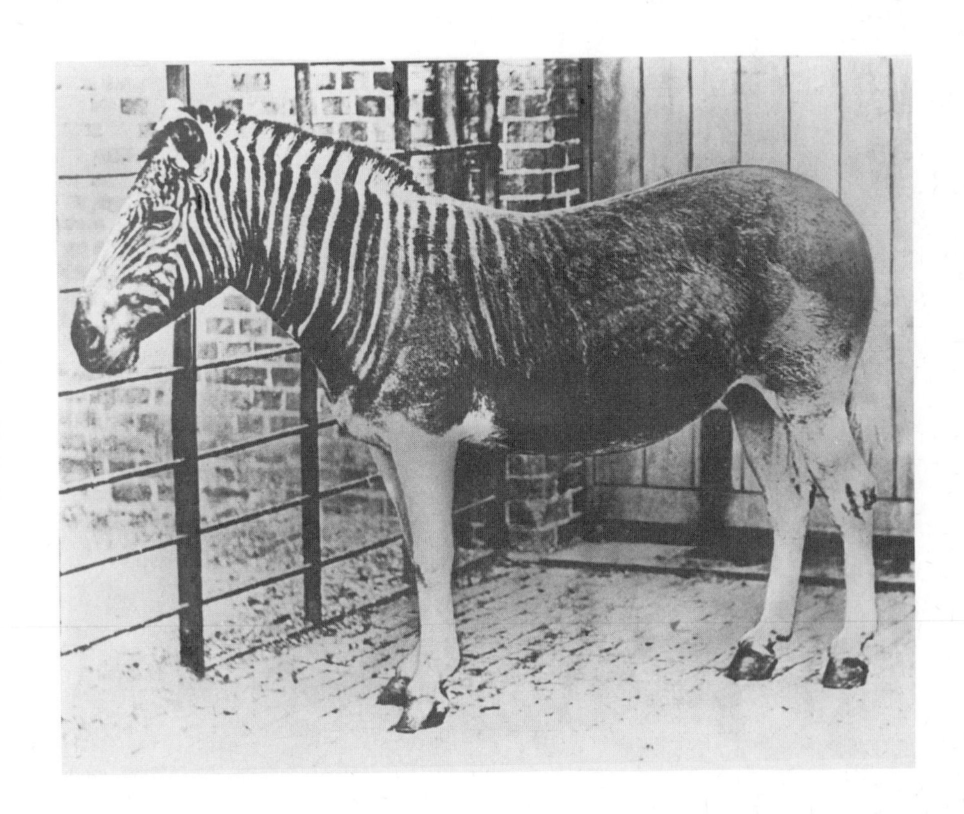

Partly because of its weird appearance, the aye-aye (*Daubentonia madagascariensis*) is regarded as an evil omen by the villagers of the East coast rainforest of Madagascar. Ritual killings and deforestation have brought the species to the verge of extinction, and very few specimens have been kept in captivity since this photograph was taken in 1913

The kagu, found only in New Caledonia (1921). This shy, heron-like bird is the sole representative of its family, and it is now threatened with extinction

Like many other forest-living mammals in Madagascar, the fossa (*Cryptoprocta ferox*) is now quite rare. It is the largest of the Madagascar carnivore species, all of which are related to civet cats (1913)

R. I. Pocock, Superintendent from 1903 to 1923, with a kinkajou (1923)

Frederick Martin Duncan (right) with Dr B. Barnett in 1934. Duncan was appointed Librarian and Clerk of Publications in 1919. He was an expert photographer and a leading photomicrographer of the period

Mr J. Young, head gardener, at his retirement in 1921

Dr F. P. Stowell, first Curator of the Aquarium, with Mr L. C. Bushby, Curator of Insects, in 1927

Performing chimpanzees were once one of the main attractions for the public at London Zoo. The chimpanzees' tea-party and other events have now been discontinued so that the chimpanzees can be kept in more natural breeding groups. *Below* Chimpanzees' tea-party (1928). *Left* Two chimps with sun shade (1931). *Right* Chimpanzees dining in style (1934). *Bottom right* Chimpanzees' tea-party (1932)

Cleaning up after the August bank holiday, 1924